HISTORY CORNER

Ancient Romans

Alice Harman

WAYLAND

Explore the world with **Popcorn -** your complete first non-fiction library.

Look out for more titles in the Popcorn range. All books have the same format of simple text and striking images. Text is carefully matched to the pictures to help readers to identify and understand key vocabulary.
www.waylandbooks.co.uk/popcorn

First published in 2012 by Wayland
Copyright © Wayland 2012

Wayland
Hachette Children's Books
338 Euston Road
London NW1 3BH

Wayland Australia
Level 17/207 Kent Street
Sydney NSW 2000

Produced for Wayland by
White-Thomson Publishing Ltd
www.wtpub.co.uk
+44 (0)843 208 7460

Editor: Alice Harman
Designer: Clare Nicholas
Picture researcher: Alice Harman
Series consultant: Kate Ruttle
Design concept: Paul Cherrill

British Library Cataloguing in Publication Data
Harman, Alice.
   Romans. -- (History corner)(Popcorn)
   1. Rome--Civilization--Juvenile literature. 2. Rome--
History--Juvenile literature.
   I. Title II. Series
   937-dc23

   ISBN: 978 0 7502 6732 8

Wayland is a division of Hachette Children's Books,
an Hachette UK company.
www.hachette.co.uk

Printed and bound in China

Picture/illustration credits: Alamy: North Wind Picture
Archives 6/9, The Art Archive 10, Lebrecht Music and
Arts Photo Library 14; Peter Bull 23; Stefan Chabluk 4;
Corbis: National Geographic Society 13, David Lees
17, Araldo de Luca 21; Mary Evans: Mary Evans Picture
Library 10, INTERFOTO / Sammlung Rauch 16; Getty:
De Agostini 18; Wikimedia: Ad Meskens 5, Andreas
Wahra 7, Fabien Dany 11, Wikimedia 12, Marie-Lan
Nguyen 15, Marie-Lan Nguyen 19, Andrew Bossi 20

Every effort has been made to clear copyright.
Should there be any inadvertent omission,
please apply to the publisher for rectification.

 Contents

Who were the ancient Romans?

The ancient Romans came from Italy. For hundreds of years, they ruled most of Europe and parts of Asia and Africa.

The land that the Romans ruled over was called the Roman Empire.

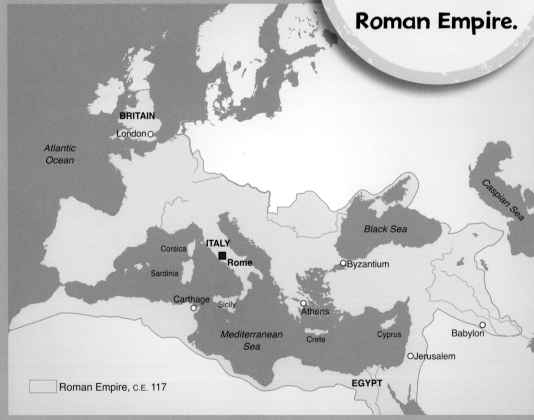

BRITAIN
Londono
Atlantic Ocean
Caspian Sea
Black Sea
Corsica
ITALY
■ Rome
oByzantium
Sardinia
Carthage
o
Sicily
Athens
o
Cyprus
Babylon
o
Mediterranean Sea
Crete
oJerusalem
EGYPT
☐ Roman Empire, C.E. 117

The ancient Romans lived between 2,750 and 1,600 years ago. They built forts, roads and buildings all over the Roman Empire.

The Romans built this bridge in France. It carries water from one place to another.

Roman leaders

Julius Caesar was a famous Roman leader. He travelled to different countries and won many battles.

This painting shows Julius Caesar leading his soldiers into battle.

Augustus was the adopted son of Julius Caesar. He was the first Roman leader who was called an emperor.

Augustus ruled over the Roman Empire for around 40 years.

The months of July and August are named after Julius Caesar and Augustus.

At home

In the cities, rich Roman families lived in houses that were built on one floor. Most people lived in blocks of flats called *insulae*.

Rich people decorated their houses with columns and statues.

statue

column

In the countryside, rich people had large houses called villas. Many servants and slaves worked in Roman villas, taking care of the owners.

These slaves are carrying the villa owner around his huge garden.

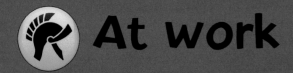

At work

Ancient Romans from rich families owned big farms. Poorer people and slaves worked on the farms to produce food.

There were lots of different plants and animals to look after on large farms.

Women worked in the house and cared for the children. Some women worked on farms or in shops. There were also many women who were slaves.

Some women were servants to rich ladies. They helped them to wash and dress.

Food

Most Romans ate fresh, simple food. They liked fruits and vegetables, meat and fish, grains and oils. They often cooked with herbs and spices.

This picture shows some of the foods that rich Romans had for dinner.

olives

prawns

Rich Romans had large and expensive dinner parties. They ate six or seven main courses of food, followed by several types of dessert.

Romans burped while eating a meal to show that they liked the food!

At dinner parties, Romans often lay on their stomachs around the table.

13

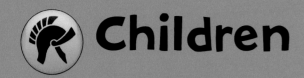 # Children

Some boys in ancient Rome went to school from the age of about seven until eleven. Most girls and poor children did not go to school.

Roman schools were very small. In most schools, there was only one teacher.

Most boys and girls played with toys such as board games and dolls. Some children had toys such as kites, hoops and stilts.

Rich children sometimes had ducks, pigeons or monkeys as pets!

This stone carving shows boys playing a game using walnuts.

Clothes and jewellery

Most Roman men wore simple clothes made of wool. Rich men sometimes wore large pieces of folded cloth, called togas. Women wore long, loose dresses.

Togas were often white, and very heavy to wear. Poor people were not allowed to wear togas.

Rich women wore lots of jewellery, including necklaces, rings, earrings and bracelets. Jewellery was often made from gold, and sometimes with precious stones such as sapphires.

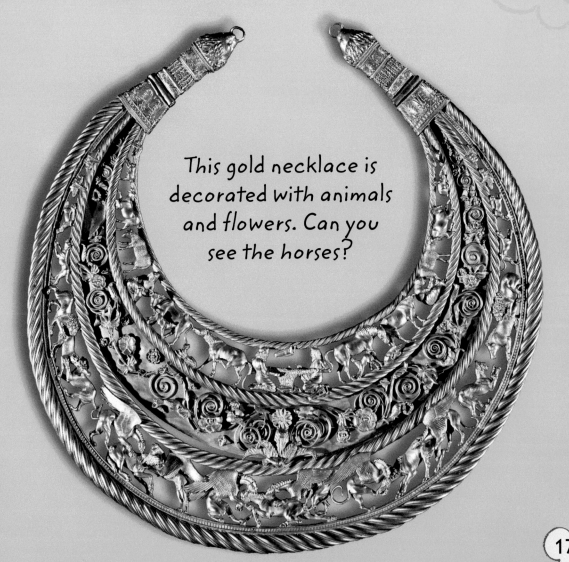

This gold necklace is decorated with animals and flowers. Can you see the horses?

Fun and leisure

The ancient Romans liked chariot racing. In this sport, men drove small carts pulled by four horses. It was fast and exciting, but very dangerous.

Chariot races took place in large buildings. People watched from the sides of the racetrack.

In ancient Rome, lots of people went to the theatre to watch funny or serious plays. The actors in these plays often wore masks and costumes on stage.

How many masks can you find in this picture of a Roman play?

Gods and beliefs

The ancient Romans believed in many gods and goddesses. Jupiter was king of the gods. He was also god of the sky.

Jupiter is often shown with an eagle. It is a sign of his power.

The planets in our solar system are named after ancient Roman gods.

Countries that became part of the Roman Empire had their own gods. Sometimes, the ancient Romans began to believe in these gods themselves.

Many ancient Romans prayed to Isis. Isis was the ancient Egyptian goddess of mothers.

Roman numerals

The Romans counted using letters from their alphabet. These letters were put together in different ways to make numbers.

All the numbers between 1 and 10 were written using the letters I, V and X.

On the right, you can see the Roman numerals that match up with the numbers we use today.

Try to do some sums using Roman numerals!

1	I	2	II
3	III	4	IV
5	V	6	VI
7	VII	8	VIII
9	IX	10	X

VI + II = ?

VI + IV = ?

X – V = ?

Answers: top = VIII (8); middle = X (10); bottom = V (5)

Make a mosaic

You will need:
- black paper or card
- coloured paper
(a few different colours)
- pencil · scissors
- glue stick

The Romans used tiny pieces of stone, and sometimes glass and ceramic, to create pictures. These pictures are called mosaics. Roman houses and other buildings had mosaics on their floors and walls.

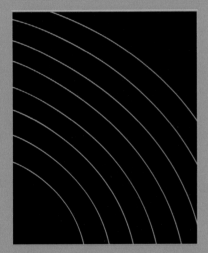

1. Use your pencil to draw a simple picture on your black paper or card. You could draw a rainbow, a sun or maybe a flower.

2. Decide which colours you'd like to use in your mosaic. Cut the coloured paper into strips, and then into small squares.

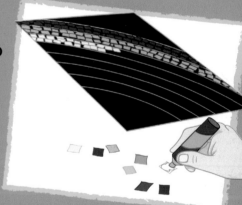

3. Put glue on the back of the small squares and stick them onto the black card. Completely fill in your drawing with these coloured squares to create your own mosaic!

Visit our website to download larger, printable templates for this project.
www.waylandbooks.co.uk/popcorn

Glossary

adopted someone who is adopted is cared for by someone who isn't their birth parent

battle a fight between two big groups of people

column a tall, upright post that supports a building or structure

emperor a man who rules over a group of countries

empire a group of countries that have the same ruler

enemy someone who you don't like, and who doesn't like you

fort a building like a castle, specially built to protect people from attacks

planet a round object that moves in a circle around a star

racetrack an area of ground, usually a large loop, where races are held

servant someone who works in another person's house, helping them in return for money

slave someone who works for no money, and is not free

solar system the Sun and the planets and other objects that move around it

stilts a pair of poles with places to put your feet on, so you can walk high off the ground

wool the hair of a sheep, made into fabric for clothes and other uses

Index

EXPLORE THE WORLD WITH THE POPCORN NON-FICTION LIBRARY!

Popcorn

- Develops children's knowledge and understanding of the world by covering a wide range of topics in a fun, colourful and engaging way
- Simple sentence structure builds readers' confidence
- Text checked by an experienced literacy consultant and primary deputy-head teacher
- Closely matched pictures and text enable children to decode words
- Includes a cross-curricular activity in the back of each book

WATCH OUT!
ear Water
Honor Head

HISTORY CORNER
The Great Fire of London
Jenny Powell

SCIENCE CORNER
Sound and Hearing
Angela Royston

FAMILIES
My Mum
Katie Dicker

GOOD FOOD
Vegetables
Julia Adams

PEOPLE WHO HELP US
Police
Honor Head

PEOPLE WHO HELP US
irefighters

GEOGRAPHY CORNER
Rainforests
Ruth Thomson

A YEAR OF FESTIVALS
Muslim Festivals
Eid Mubarak! Nasreen Hasid

HISTORY CORNER
The Gunpowder Plot
Jenny Powell

IN SPACE
Planets
Chris Oxlade

SEASONS
Winter
Kay Barnham

FREE DOWNLOADS!

OVER 50 TITLES TO CHOOSE FROM!

- Written by an experienced teacher
- Learning objectives clearly marked
- Provides information on where the books fit into the curriculum
- Photocopiable so pupils can take them home

www.waylandbooks.co.uk/downloads